France in Ruins

Buildings in decay

Simon O'Corra

GHP

This title is published by
Golden House Publications

Printed in the UK

by

CPI Antony Rowe
Bumper's Farm
Chippenham
Wiltshire SN14 6LH

London 2011

ISBN 978-1-906137-23-6

Dedicated to my partner Nigel Bray for his unstinting love and support during the writing of this book.

Contents

Foreword

'"*Our sharing with our fellows is a human insight into the ruin and the ruin's insight into humanity, for we are still looking at things from the ruin's point of view. The ruin examines its visitors and puts them to the test by diverse exercises. We see them doing what the ruin has set forth for them to do. They crane their necks and look up at us. We are a tower.* '[1]

Around every corner in France can be found a ruin, these mysterious things which we are encouraged to notice and seek a closer look at. These edifices may be: an old barn attached to a long forgotten farmhouse; an old school or factory; a faded old chateau no longer reverberating with the sound of the leisured classes at play or an old church long since bereft of the spoken or sung Mass. Ruins can be symbols of decay, financial depression or family feuds, whilst others are living coin-operated revenue-building exercises, presented in conjunction with a kind of faux historicism, the *spectacle.* This brand of theatre juxtaposes clinically conserved ruined buildings in a *mise en scene* with a lavishly costumed extravaganza peopled by local volunteers, many of whom may have little idea of the incongruity of their actions within a now non-working building. Currently this can be seen in many cities, towns and villages in France. The former, those ruins of neglect, do not need a theatrical input, as their structures present and express histories, dramas and romances, and thereby enable an anthropomorphism to occur, one fashioned by each viewer.

One might have expected that in France, as in the United States, that a study of ruined buildings at any given time might reveal mostly relatively modern decaying buildings, waiting for demolition to be followed by a swift rebuild or even a new development. On the contrary, in France, during the last year as I sought out ruins, only two buildings have actually been restored to their former use and glory: a small house, and a chateau converted into flats. Also most of the ruins in this book have been ruined and deserted for many many years, if not centuries, and yet they still exist, despite the ravages of time and the vagaries of the weather and nature. Here in France we see not a random and ever changing process of ruination and rebuilding, but a definitive Culture of Ruination.

This book examines the ruins of France, both visually and in terms of defining them and the culture which has made, and continues to make, them. The photographs provide both representations of ruins in detail, which in some cases show us the process of decay and also larger scale images, setting ruins in their surrounding landscapes, which can provide insights into the reasons for ruination. The text focusses on the roots of dereliction, the history of the genre in art and literature, the background to individual ruins where possible, the psychology which can underpin human response to ruins and the social and economic impact of ruins in contemporary society in France.

Simon O'Corra (17th January 2011)

[1] *The Aesthetics of Ruins, Ginsberg, Robert,* Amsterdam/New York, 2004, 182

Picture credits

Chapter 1
Debbie Jenkin - Fig.1
Simon O'Corra - Fig.2, Fig.7, Fig.8, Fig.10, Fig.11, Fig.12
Linda Pennin - Fig.3
Postcard - Fig.4, Fig.5, Fig.9
Alf Emil Eik - Fig.6,

Chapter 2
Debbie Jenkin - Fig.1, Fig.4, Fig.6
John Light - Fig.2, Simon O'Corra - Fig.3
Anne Patterson - Fig.5, Postcards - Fig.7,

Chapter 3
Postcards - Fig. 1, Fig.3, Fig.6, Fig.7
World War One Colour Photos - Fig.2, Fig.4, Fig.5

Chapter 4.
Simon O'Corra Fig. 1, 2, 3, 4, 5, 6, 7, 8, 9, 12, 22, 23, 24, 33, 34, 35, 36, 37, 60
Debbie Jenkin Fig.10, 29, 30, 31, 32, 38, 39, 40, 41, 42, 43, 44, 45, 46, 47, 48, 49, 50, 51, 52, 53, 54, 55, 56, 57, 58, 59
Tara Bradford Fig.11, 25, 26, 27, 28
Linda Pennin Fig.13, 17
John Light Fig.14, 18, 19, 20
Anne Patterson Fig.15,16
Postcard Fig.21Michel
Levoye Fig.61, 62, 63, 64, 65, 66, 67, 68, 69, 70, 71, 72, 73, 74, 75, 76, 77, 78, 79, 80, 81

Chapter 5
Simon O'Corra - Fig.1, 2, 3, 4, 5, 6, 7, 8, 9, 10, 11, 12, 13, 14, 15, 16, 17, 18, 23, 24, 31, 32, 33, 36, 37, 38, 39, 40, 41, 42, 43, 44, 45, 46, 47, 48, 49, 50, 51, 52, 53, 54
Debbie Jenkin - Fig.19, 20,21,22, 25, 26, 27, 28, 29, 30, 34, 35
Michel Levoye - Fig.55, 56, 57, 58, 59

Chapter 6
Simon O'Corra - Fig. 1, 2, 3, 4, 5, 6, 7, 8. 9, 10, 11, 12, 13
John Hugh Parker - Fig.14 and 15
John Light - Fig.16
Debbie Jenkin - Fig.17, 18
Michel Levoye - Fig.19 and 20

Chapter 7
Simon O'Corra - Fig.1, 2, 3, 4, 5, 6, 7, 8, 9, 10, 11, 12, 13, 15, 16, 17, 18, 19, 20, 21,22, 23, 24, 25, 26, 27, 28, 29, 30, 31, 32, 33
Lucien Moerkamp - Fig.14,
Michel Levoye - 34, 35, 36, 37, 38, 39

Chapter 8
Debbie Jenkin - Fig.1, 2, 3, 4, 5, 6, 7,

Chapter 9
Simon O'Corra - Fig. 1, 2, 4, 5, 6, 7, 8, 9
John Light - Fig.3

Chapter 10 Christophe Bonvarlet - Fig.1,
Postcards - Fig.2, 3, 4, 5, 6, 7
Matthew Smith - Fig.8
Simon O'Corra - Fig.9, 10

Chapter 1 - Ruination and Desertion: Interpretation and Basis

> *"You don't know" he said, "why ruins give so much pleasure..." I will tell you... Everything dissolves, everything perishes, everything passes, only time goes on... How old the world is. I walk between two eternities ...What is my existence in comparison with this crumbling stone?"*[1]

Fig. 1 Chateau Villedieu

For the purpose of this book, the interpretation of a ruin is either a) a building which has been deserted and uninhabited for many years and/or b) a building which is in a parlous and even dangerous state due to neglect and therefore uninhabitable. You will see here ruined chateaux, houses, factories, schools, railway stations, religious buildings and farm buildings. Some may be open to the public as commercial touristic ruins and others have been frozen in a certain time, as the situations of their owners have changed. Some are prey to nature like Chateau Villedieu and Chateau Le Pin, (Fig. 1 & Fig. 2). It is impossible to truly attempt to define 'ruins'. They, each one of them, defy classification. Each has its own story, and many such stories will be explored in this book. There is also no single basis for there being ruined and deserted buildings in France. Throughout Europe one can still see ruins, especially as a result of the First and Second World Wars. But France, it seems, is unique in the sheer *number* of its ruins. Of course there is, particularly in small towns, a range of houses to be found which are not ruined but are still nevertheless deserted by their owners, kept locked up and seemingly forgotten. They are, thankfully, often held together by those houses which abut them. This chapter however, focuses on the former types of buildings which are both ruined *and* deserted.

[1] Rose Macaulay, *Pleasure of Ruins, a conversation between Denis Diderot, writer and Hubert Robert, painter,* London 1953, 23

Fig. 2 Chateau Le Pin

What descriptors can be used in the culture of ruination? What follows is a far from exhaustive list: decay, disintegration, disrepair, dilapidation, ruination, destruction, demolition, wreckage, remains, remnants, fragments, relics, rubble, debris, wreckage, downfall, collapse, devastation, lay-waste, raze, wipe out, flatten, dereliction, tumbledown, ramshackle, decrepit, ruinous, parlous. This fulsome list is perhaps indicative of a general inability to pin ruined buildings down as a single genre or type.

Fig. 3 Chateau Tours D'Aigue

A few obvious motivations for ruination and desertion are:

i) **War** - Like many European countries, France has had a warring and turbulent past. It has also engaged in violent civil wars. Siege warfare was the *modus operandi* of many such conflicts and was used to break down the opponent's resolve and as a result, in many cases, totally destroyed buildings by the means of a constant bombardment. In 1789 the French Revolution also had a devastating effect on the country's infrastructure in terms both of civic and private buildings (Fig. 3). There was, for a brief period, a wanton disregard for the property of others, particularly of the aristocracy and the Church. However, the result of the revolution was that mans' inalienable right to property was secured in the constitution. For the first time, a man could take pride in his own property and be secure in, except in extreme circumstances, his and his family's ongoing ownership of it. After the revolution with the advent of Napoleon and his grandiose scheme to rule Europe and beyond, France experienced yet another period of devastation as she was invaded by foreign armies and subsequently beaten into submission, at an extreme cost to its buildings and people. Following the defeat of Napoleon, France once again faced a series of governments, both monarchical and republican, attended by violent clashes at the times of transition between them. The War with Germany in 1870 and the actions of the invading force were both cruel and vindictive, as France was overrun and devastated by the German Army, over and above what would be deemed fair and just. Paris was itself almost completely destroyed and the German Army left a trail of ruination everywhere it went, of which more in Chapter 3 (Fig. 4).

Fig. 4 Franco Prussian War Damage

A major impact on subsequent ruination and desertion in recent times in France is The First World War. The Western Front was located within France for the duration of the War and as a result, Northern France experienced a gratuitous annihilation of its buildings as all sides battled for supremacy on French soil. The conflict was barbarous and had new modern weapons which could wreak devastation on buildings. (Fig.5 1st World War photo). France had to put in place a programme of rebuilding for over 3000 villages and small towns, which it did in 1916. Still some buildings were not covered by this programme and many hamlets may have fallen into decay and ruin, rather like those small hamlets that disappeared or fell into ruin during the Potato Famine of 1848-49 in Ireland, being places too insignificant to qualify for renewal.

Buildings also suffered in the Second World War. The Chateau de Rastignac was badly damaged in 1944 as a fleeing German SS revenge squad tried to demolish it. More than 100 years of history were nearly wiped out. The grand structure was defaced and set ablaze (Fig.6 Chateau de Rastignac). The chateau is now an empty shell which has been roofed over.

> *"They torched it with gasoline and phosphorus and the fires burned for two weeks," the proprietor told me. "All furnishings and tapestries went up, leaving only the walls. It was a real tragedy. These punitive SS squads were sadistic criminals with a total lack of humanity."*[1]

[1] http://www.thecolumnists.com/johnson/johnson103.html

Fig. 5 First World War Damage

Fig. 6 Chateau Rastignac - Speculation abounds about the possible influence of this chateau on The White House in the United States. It is clear that Thomas Jefferson may have visited Rastignac in his tour of 1789, just prior to the Revolution. He was elected President in 1801 and work began on the south portico and columns in 1806.

ii) Inheritance Laws - The Laws for inheritance in France are complicated and subject to many variables. The law is very restrictive. A proportion of the estate, the *réserve legale*, must be given to specified categories of heirs: firstly, to the children and issue, and if there are no children or issue, then parents or, finally, grandparents if there are no surviving parents. The amount they can claim will take into consideration the value of gifts given to them during their lifetime.

The situation as regards *héritiers réservataires* (heir reserves) is as follows: If you are survived by one child, you can bequeath no more than half your French property; If you are survived by two children, this limit drops to one third; If you are survived by three or more children, you can only give away a quarter of your French property; If you have no children, other members of your family may qualify as legal heirs and so enjoy mandated rights to a proportion of the property. A husband or wife is not considered a legal heir and has no right to the legal reserves.

Once a group of children or parents or grandparents or multiples thereof have possession of a relative's house, the situation becomes even more complicated and has a greater impact on a building's future safety and security. In French law, where more than one person owns a building all parties must agree to the building's sale and/or renovation, and in terms of renovation all parties must agree to share the cost. It easy to understand how a building may suffer due to a group of people who cannot agree on its future. Therefore a building is in danger of being deserted and ruined by this impasse.

Another legal issue which impacts on the future of a building is a French law which relates to demolition. The *Demand de Permis de Demolir* is the documentation relating to a law put in place to prevent the demolition of a building located within a sector protected under the architectural, urban or landscape heritage system. So if a group of people or an individual is bequeathed or buys a property then it may be that they have no choice but to renovate or desert the building, thereby making another ruin. The inability to afford to renovate is discussed later.

iii) Popular Culture - Some ruined buildings have become victims, or some would say beneficiaries, of popular culture. These are buildings which have been converted to places of historical significance because of their ruined status. It is possible to make the case for both victimisation and beneficence, as these buildings have lost their living heart as habitable places and yet have not been completely lost to the world, as many places have been over the centuries. It is safe to assume that most interested people would rather see a well kept ruin than no building at all.

Fig. 7 Chateau Levroux - The castle was ratified as belonging to Richard I (*Couer de Lion*) of England in 1189.

Fig. 8 Chateau Levroux

Fig. 9 Abbey de Jumage, Normandy Northern France

iv) Romance - There is also, in France and beyond, a romantic culture of ruination and a sentimental protectiveness of all things French. Balzac's 1842 novel '*La Grande Breteche*', explores the ruined building of the same name's ability to seduce Doctor Bianchon, because the house is home to Madame de Merret's intimate secrets of seduction and betrayal. So it seems that ruins are not simply deserted and neglected wrecks but objects of romance and seduction, a fact which helps to maintain the ruination culture in France. Annette Larson Benert, refers to the First World War writings of Edith Wharton;

"Wharton's writings about the war, however, are rarely so overtly racist, or so focused on personal atrocities. Instead, they portray, rather literally, "man as a defenceless animal", thrust not simply out of necessary shelter but out of the buildings and grounds that make human life and relationships possible. The waging of World War I displaced people, destroyed farms and villages, made rubble of institutions, made the earth itself less habitable. In particular, the historic architecture of France, valued both as evidence of high civilization and as civilizing in its effects, became suddenly, frighteningly vulnerable. When news spread of cathedrals, town halls, towns themselves flattened in minutes, and of men trapped in filthy trenches and murdered or mutilated outside them by weapons of terrible force and accuracy, many otherwise sane Anglo-Americans retreated into the most primitive kind of racism."[1]

This Romantic culture, mentioned above, may be so buried within the French psyche as to be unrecognisable by individual French men and women. It may also explain why there has been ambivalence towards the respect due to buildings which do so express a country's culture. However, in the hearts and minds of many non-French people this ambivalence shapes the Romantic and sentimental culture and perhaps in some way imposes it on France and the French as a whole. The expression of ruined France in art and in literature will both be discussed in the next chapter, but here it is particularly worth noting the culture of ruination in literature which we have begun above in the work of Edith Wharton and Ralph Adams Cram below. In 1914, Ralph Adams Cram, the gothic revivalist architect, wrote a bitter account of the bombing of French Cathedrals in December 1914, detailing his view that the buildings were destroyed by a

"*new thing in the world built on all that the buildings denied.*"[2]

This statement once again provides a benediction to ruined buildings. It is a recognition of times gone by, of a new world order bent on destruction to oil the wheels of Free Trade and Capitalism. If we have no ruins through wear and tear we must create some and call it fighting for democracy and with God on our side. Of course Cram, an artist and an ecclesiastical one at that, may be biased and as a classically trained 19th century gentleman may have had little time for Modernism, brought about at such a high price.

Fig. 10 a small farmer's cottage in La Maison Mère, Indre

v) Apathy, neglect and disaster - Ruined buildings can sometimes be victims of apathy, economic constrictions and tragedies. Some buildings can be left to rot because it is easier that way, e.g. when a person inherits a house 900 km away in another part of France or when a building is no longer used for anything or when a person dies

[1] Annette Larson, Edith Wharton at War; civilised space in troubled times, Benert, *Twentieth Century Literature*, Vol. 42, 1996, 323

[2] Annette Larson Benert, Edith Wharton at War, Ralph Adams Cram account, 1996 (http://www.questia.com/googleScholar.qst?docId=5000458478)

intestate with no known relatives. There is however, a recognisable culture of maintaining the grounds of a ruin, which seems odd, but maybe people think that by keeping nature at bay that the house will look after itself, However, a deserted building has much more to contend with than just nature.

Sometimes a person inherits a house and is financially unable to renovate the place. The story behind the building in Fig. 10 is a point in question. This house once owned by the current owners great Aunt Alphonsine was bequeathed to her nephew, the present owner's father in 1958. Alphonsine had been there since 1929. At the time of the end her tenure, the house was already neglected and run down, and the nephew who already had a house nearby was not in a position to renovate what was for him an extra house. The house therefore, over the last 50 years, has been shut up and allowed to become a store for such things as old stoves and furniture and barrels belonging to the Alphonsine's brother who had been a cooper.

Fig. 11 An antique market in Levroux, Indre Department

Tragedies too can often befall old houses and places of business, as the buildings themselves are most often timber framed and by their very nature old and dried out. The shop you can see in Fig. 11, fell victim to a fire and has since begun to collapse despite being on the high street in a small town. It is cordoned off with railings which impinge on the footpath as its roof sinks into its interior. The small house in Fig 12, was also a victim of fire but has subsequently been planted out by the local commune to form a flower bed as it looks out onto a car park.

Fig. 12 A small house in St. Aignan

vi) A psychological imperative - On a collective conscious level perhaps ruins are created because we wish them to be. We may need them in some way to mirror our anxieties and fears about our own decay and dilapidation. Alternatively, as the original builders of these edifices, humans may simply wish to exercise the the right to neglect and desert the very same buildings that they so lovingly created.

The definition and basis for ruination is becoming a little clearer and will become more so as this book unfolds. Also the cure for ruins, if one is possible given the human fascination for them, is a constantly developing phenomenon as technological advancement enables more ruins to be restored and re-developed, despite their complete collapse. Equally our desire for the past and for quality affordable housing and commercial properties means that ruins are beginning to take on an increased importance in mainstream culture and are created sometimes at an even quicker pace than in the past.

Chapter 2 - Depictions of Ruination in Art and in Literature

> "*My paintings comment on the melancholy beauty found in relics of our recent industrial past. The relics remind us that, in our rapidly changing world, the triumphs of technology are just a moment away from obsolescence. Yet these remains of collapsed power have a strength, grace and sadness that is both eloquent and impenetrable.*"[1]

Ruination in Art

The comments from Anna Held Audette, and the similarity between her work and that of Hubert Robert, an 18th century painter of ruins, indicates that she, as with other artists who have produced 'ruined building' paintings have, as their inspiration and creative *raison d'etre*, a heterogeneous range of issues, despite being part of a sub-classification in art, that of the 'ruined building expressives'. Anna Audette is the latest in a long line of ruin devotees who have used, and continue to use, ruined buildings to explore and explain their world to others, despite there often being different motivations at play.

The West's view of ruins is a conglomeration of romanticism and sentimentalism, mixed over time with the violence occasioned by war which reached its apogee during the First World War. Alternatively, for instance, in Pre-Modern China, the expression of ruins in visual art had been proscribed, finding an outlet only in poetry, but in 19th century China depictions of ruins became fashionable as 'photographic propaganda', meant to instill in the viewer a fear of foreign intervention and hostilities. These propaganda images are a kind of demolition ruin, similar to that of Anne Held Audette although present in two widely differing cultures. An example of this demolition ruin in China is the Old Summer Palace or Imperial Gardens outside Beijing which were ironically entirely destroyed by French troops in 1860 but are still revered by the Chinese as a reminder of foreign hostilities. Diderot was right when in 1765 he maintained that a palace was only to be revealed as of interest by destroying it.

As this book is focussed on ruined buildings in France I will discuss the culture of ruination as it has manifested itself in European Art, from the 18th century onwards. For example, prior to the French Revolution, Giovanni Battista Piranesi (1720-1778), was developing a small *oeuvre* of Roman ruins in his art. Unlike his younger contemporaries Hubert Robert, previously mentioned, and Charles Louis Clerisseau , his depiction of ruins with attendant and contemporary human subjects was often a foil for the human condition, a melancholic expression as analogous as it is representational. The details in Piranesi's Ruin Paintings differ from his contemporaries in that his were often a conglomeration of fragments rather than complete topographical representations. However, all of these artists can trace a lineage back to Giovanni Paulo Pannini, a Baroque *Quadratura* or purely illusionistic painter. With Robert and Clerisseau, an altogether younger generation of artists, came the development of a ruin capriccio style: a mix of fantasy and reality.

The depictions of ruination in art were often of ancient ruins mostly pre-dating the Medieval period, but have nevertheless impacted on the development of a culture of ruin across the building styles within France since the Revolution. With the advent of the Grand Tour for young Englishmen and women in the nineteenth century, this culture of ruination in France, and to an extent elsewhere, found tacit romantic and sentimental approval from a large part of the English speaking world. Individuals brought paintings of ruins back to their country estates and then began to create fake ruined follies there, e.g. Robert Adams, Poultney Bridge in Bath, thereby reinventing the culture out of its geographical context. This romantic notion for ruination has enabled individuals, local communes and central government in France to leave buildings to fall into ruination when it was not practical or financially possible to repair them, safe in the knowledge that they will not be judged for doing so. All of this adds to the mystique of France, and its unique place in the hearts of the many peoples of the world.

France has had much destruction visited upon its land and buildings over the last two hundred years and a concomitant outpouring of visual representation of ruination. These representations are symbolic of the ever changing moral and political climate in France. One painting, *'La Bourse ou La Vie'*, by Joseph Louis Hippolyte Bellange (c.1827), is a social commentary on the times, overshadowed as the action of the piece is, by an enormous and powerful looking ruin, symbolic of the old ways, steadfastly and resolutely holding its ground, despite the moral decay around it, as expressed by the hoards of marauding bourgeoisie and peasantry. Another example, *'A Book on a Plinth by a Rose Bush at the Ruins'* by Simon Saint Jean (1808-1860) is an unusual

[1] Anna Held Audette (personal communication, 2008)

almost *surreal*, still life and landscape. It raises all sorts of questions, about why the artists has used such a complex arrangement of everyday objects and set them in a ruined environment. Is it perhaps a master class in art, a means for the artist to show his virtuosity? The other possible explanation could be an allegorical one, explaining the frailties of nature and of man's understanding of life. At a later date a change of style can be witnessed in the work of J. Skene, depicting the Mosque inside the ruins of the Parthenon, a juxtaposing of ancient dilapidation with new build utilisation. This is something which is still to be seen in current ruins in France.

As we move through the nineteenth century, painted images of ruins give way to photographic images. As the photograph forms the larger part of the rest of this volume, we will be reviewing photographic representations of ruination in later chapters and here we must for the sake of ease and to avoid a lengthy debate about the photograph as art form, leave this technique and move on to ruination in sculpture and arts installations.

> "*It is quite true that an aesthetic consideration of decay cannot impose a rigid analysis onto something wholly ambiguous. Decay resists and alters its form before it can be dissected as such.*"[1]

In the 1970's and 1980's, SITE inc, (Sculpture in the Environment), an arts corporation, focussed its attention on the fragility and ephemeral nature of buildings, most certainly human constructs. Two startling examples of their work which epitomise and reaffirm this book's expression and definition of ruination are:

> "*The Tilt Showroom (built in 1978 in Towson, Maryland) was particularly humorous, featuring an entire front facade tipped up at an absurd angle. The large building was transformed visually into a child's toy, broken and discarded.*"[2]

The other being:

> "*The impression of sudden disaster provided by these showrooms resonated with another theme common in SITE's work—that of nature consuming human artifice. This concept was first fully realized in the Best Forest Building (1980, Richmond, Virginia), which incorporated surrounding trees into the body of the structure.*"[3]

This process of ruination is not an uncommon sight in this work as so many ruins are seen to be being reclaimed by nature (see Fig. 94, Chapter 4). Not only are these sculptural and architectural installations expressions of ruination but also, like the neglect and desertion of ruins in France, they are 'creations' of ruins, the basis for the Ruins Culture. All ruined buildings are created through 'performative structures' and SITE inc. are also exponents thereof, despite using artificial constructs to explain the human's relation to its buildings and to nature. These installations, like real ruined buildings, are created, because even neglect and desertion are creations of a kind, as they have intent behind them.

Ruination in Literature

A surprisingly large and rich body of literature exists both theoretical and fictional, both attempting an analysis of the culture of ruination and also a description of ruins themselves. These theories and accounts are limitless. This chapter seeks to present just a few examples of these two methods of hypothesis and descriptive texts concerning ruined buildings. Dylan Trigg speaks of the cultural ambiguity of ruins, each one it seems having at its root a disparate creation point and erosional development. This 'creation' of ruin, which can occur for romantic, sentimental or even financial reasons is on a spectrum which includes the development of ruin through a straightforward 'abandonment', a negation of care. Also time may change the look of a ruined building, but the building still maintains its ruined status, as the years go by. A ruin is a ruin and always remains so, in simple

---

1 Dylan Trigg (personal communication 2010)

2 Jessica Robey, Invisible Culture, *Internet Journal*, 2003 (http://www.pipsworks.com/crosswalk/prov04/c1dylan.html)

3 Jessica Robey, 'Appetite for Destruction:Public Iconography and the Artificial Ruins of SITE, Inc.' *Invisible culture*, 2003, 7 (https://urresearch.rochester.edu/institutionalPublicationPublicView.action?institutionalItemId=1006&versionNumber=1)

terms. Even though adjectives abound such as 'ancient', 'old', 'charming', 'derelict', the fact remains that all ruined buildings have a set of descriptors that are unchanging. It is the reasons for the ruination that are manifold. Trigg again draws a comparison between being locked in a closed and deserted shopping centre and standing in a ruin, the former a kind of temporary and exciting experience which nevertheless has very little historical meaning as the next day it will be a utilitarian and functional space once more, alive and current. The latter a space shaped by the decay of decades or centuries, with its own historical and creative dynamic.

> "*Aesthetically, the presence of decay introduces us to a narrative that the pristine space cannot afford...we find ourselves at once in a space of both presence and absence, and what then arises from this disjunctive conjunction is a sense of the uncanny.*"[1]

Within a ruin it is possible to see changes in form and decay often occasioned by the encroachment of nature and also to witness a void caused by the negation of a building's initial purpose. Rather like a magic trick, a ruin bears both descriptors within its being: 'Now you see it now you don't' or maybe you see all of it in all its glorious mystery and defiance.

Fig. 1 Chateau Le Pin

The 'uncanny' disjunctive conjunction aspect has within it a similarity to Foucault's normal/ abnormal dichotomy, which makes a ruin so seductive to many. Ruins in this context can be perversions of the 'norm', i.e. not habitable buildings, whilst at the same time, holding a place in cultural norms i.e. artistic and romantic icons that inspire. This polarity of compliance and deviance, both necessary Capitalist control mechanisms, allow ruins to survive as an emblem of our culture and paradoxically as a warning witness to depravity and dissolution - in many cases, veiled and hidden (Fig. 1). This secrecy turns them into places that must be intruded on by the curious. (Fig. 2.) This dichotomy encourages an eroticism and mystery in ruined buildings and in the feelings of the devotee. Ruins are at once a relic of a powerful past linked to cultural supremacy, mingled with daring and trangressive elements, that stand defiant against all that is modern and clean. Ruined buildings as transgressive entities challenge cultural orthodoxy with unconventional behaviour, being shelters without normal function and given the heterogeneous nature of decay, also present experimental forms in flux.

[1] Dylan Trigg , *The uncanny space of decay, (http://www.pipsworks.com/crosswalk/prov04/c1dylan.html)*

Fig. 2 The Old Mill at Jameau

Ruins are both 'dirty secrets' and also important icons of Capitalism, Power and Stoicism. In his book *'Industrial Ruins: Space, Aesthetics, and Materiality'*, Tim Edensor views industrial and other ruins, as signifiers of the failure of the Capitalist system (Fig 3) and as places still utilised by contemporary homeless humans and members of the natural kingdom, by film producers and photographers, (Fig.4) and even as adventure play-grounds. He also states that they are memorials to those people who inhabited them in their heyday, expressions of the struggles and the productivity played out within their walls. Later in this book commercial and civic buildings will be explored and shown to have just as much interest as the romantic chateau or chapel. In fact, all of the buildings in this book are exemplars of political and social change, brought about by: war, financial crises both national and global; the changes in national legislation, and because France is within the European Union, the dictates of that political grouping also.

Fig. 3 Le Blanc

Fig. 4 The artists view of Chateau Villedieu

Robert Ginsberg, in his The Aesthetics of Ruins, states that

> "*Ruins flourish as matter, form, function, incongruity, site, and symbol. Ruin underlies cultural values in cinema, literature and philosophy. Finally, ruin guides meditations upon our mortality and endangered world.*"[1]

Fig. 5 Chateau de la Mothe - Before 1650 the castle became the property of François de Rochechouart, after his role in the Fronde he was exiled and brought a considerable court with him, but by 1668 he had left the house to his creditors who sold it to his sister, Marie de Rochechouart.

---

[1] Robert Ginsberg, *The Aesthetics of Ruins,* Amsterdam/New York, 2004 (Publisher's Note reverse cover)

By contrast John Brinckerhoff Jackson states in his essay *'The Necessity for Ruins'* that ruins are actually a reflection of our nostalgia and vernacular past, rather than admiration of beauty or an event. This viewpoint is particularly witnessed in fictional literature and personal diaries which are further explored in this chapter. In some ways fictional accounts of ruination are even more evocative than those expressed in visual art. The romance of the ruin in visual images is often replaced with a starker, scarier and sadder evocation in the novel, short story or social commentary. The poignancy of a ruined building is often given free rein in the written word (Fig. 5). The ruins that are mentioned in literature are often used as analogies for other situations and more closely connected to either real people or characters and their emotions expressed in novels, personal diaries and social commentaries. People often attach clandestine and romantic attributes to the ruin. These buildings are of course generally empty, devoid of human habitation, so there is little risk that a person may come along to gainsay the onlooker's romantic viewpoint (Fig. 6). The truth is though, in works such as *La Grande Bretèche*, by Honor de Balzac, a ruin can hide a deadly secret, one that even a now dead former resident is keeping hidden from the world, through the dictates of her will.

> *"The roof of the house is horribly dilapidated, the shutters are always closed, the balconies are covered with swallows' nests, the doors are continually shut. Tall grasses have outlined in green the cracks in the doorsteps, and the ironwork is rusty...Everywhere an invisible hand has written the word Mystery"*[1]

Fig. 6 Chateau Villedieu

[1] Honoré de Balzac, *La Grande Breteche,* 1832 *(2)*, 176-177

Balzac's main character Horace Bianchon, goes on to question why this building has been left in such a dreadful condition, even suggesting France may have been betrayed in the existence of this ruin, a reflection of Tim Edensor's view that ruins express a society's capitalist failures. He also asserts that the house is a great enigma, something that many people today feel is true of contemporary ruins. Bianchon goes on to describe his feelings about the house:

> "*the sight of this dwelling place became one of my keenest pleasures.*'"[1]

The reader is left unsure as to what is the object of this pleasure. Is it the building, its sad condition or, as becomes apparent, a 'mystery' which Bianchon has to solve at all costs? Once he is told that his visits to the house are 'trespass', occasioned by the law concerning closed estates and instituted by the will of the deceased Comtesse de Merret, his romantic impulses are engaged. Can we read passion or eroticism for 'the keenest pleasure'? The incongruity of keen pleasure attached to a ruined dwelling, may indicate just that. Perhaps Bianchon is engaged in a 'forbidden fruit' type of attachment to this place, for complex and arbitrary reasons? Maybe the house is expressing a kind of 'naughty nakedness' as it begins to decay and drop its outer clothing revealing its undergarments or super structure. This once again, if true, would be a deviance from the accepted cultural norm. At this point the ruined house becomes greater than its parts, as do many ruined buildings today. The story of the house's current ruination unfolds for the rest of the story and the last words of the piece spoken by the Comte de Merret are prophetic:

> "*You swore on the cross that there was no one there*"

His words pre-empt the building's future abandonment and reflects the house's current status in the novel as an empty and closed space. As a result of the Comtesse's indiscretion, the house has remained deserted and silenced, as do many buildings today. They hide their secrets but often not very well. Home is so important to so many of us, even if it is a factory that we once owned, that the viewer/detective is often sceptical about the excuses, or lack of them, for ruination that are laid before him or her. Romantic notions aside, the other major discussion of ruins in literature is of violent or sadistic destruction occasioned by war or sometimes by individual soldiers as seen at the Chateau de Rastignac, mentioned in Chapter 1. These ruins are described in literature, at the point of destruction, therefore making ruination a performative construct, even though they may have been either flattened or rebuilt in the ensuing years. In the novel '*A Son at the Front*' by Edith Wharton, she describes the feelings of the main character, an artist living in Paris during World War One, as news of the barbarity intensified, he saw...

> *"man as a defenceless animal suddenly torn from his shell, stripped of all the interwoven tendrils of association, habit, background...flung out of the human habitable world into naked ether, where nothing breathes or lives.'"*[2]

There is no romantic mystery here but instead a genuine fear of and horror for the vulnerability of life and of buildings, mutilated and destroyed at the whim of mankind and of individual States. The war expresses the annihilation both of humanity and the glorious civilising environments that it has developed over the centuries. (Fig.7)

> *'"In particular, the historic architecture of France, valued both as evidence of high civilization and as civilizing in its effects, became suddenly, frighteningly vulnerable."*[3]

Edith Wharton was one of those fortunate Americans who travelled extensively in Europe and who had an extraordinary respect and regard for European culture and civilisation. Many Americans held France in particular regard as the arbiter of European culture and Wharton loved it so much that she settled in Paris in later life. It

[1] Honore de Balzac *La Grande Breteche,* France, 1832 *(2)*, 177

[2] Annette Benert Larson, Edith Wharton at War, A Son at the Front, 1996 (http://www.questia.com/googleScholar.qst?docId=5000458478)

[3] Annette Larson Benert, *Edith Wharton at War; civilised space in troubled times,* 1996, 1

is obvious to see why she should be so affected by the wanton destruction that she was witnessing in France as the war unfolded and also apparent what effective a tool France's enemies had in the destruction of its towns and villages, striking as it did at its national identity. Ralph Adams Cram, in a diary entry, has another view about the destruction of French Cathedrals during the first World War. He recognised a kind of replacement religion, witnessing the old civilisation built on religion being destroyed and replaced by the new religion of technology, ugliness and counter-culture. He thought that these beautiful buildings represented the views of a civilised society which hitherto had denied the very essence of this new religion of ruination. It is interesting though that ruins now have a romantic life of their own, perhaps as they are separated from the cause of ruination by many years.

What is clear is that an attempt to postulate on and chronicle ruins and the culture within which they sit is also an extremely difficult and potentially never-ending process. If it is possible to pinpoint a definitive theory for ruined buildings at a given time, by the time a hypothesis or definition reaches the press, the theoretical base could have shifted with the times or a ruin could have deteriorated further or, as in the case of some houses in France, been rebuilt completely, thus re-inventing a modern version on an historical theme.

Fig. 7 Rheims Cathedral - The cathedral church of Notre-Dame de Rheims is where the Kings of France were once crowned. The present building sits on the site of an ancient basilica where King Clovis was crowned in AD 496. The cathedral suffered extensive damage in the First World War but with generous support from the Rockerfeller family it was restored and re-opened in 1938.

Chapter 3 - War Devastation and Ruination

> *"Wrecks wetly mouldering under rain, Everywhere. Remember Belgium!"*[1]

Although France has a long history of warfare, it was the period between the Religious Wars (1530-1610) and the French Revolution (1789-1799) that brought about the culture of ruination, as we know it today. This in part is because both of these conflicts involved French people on both sides and involved two of the strongest imperatives for conflict and retribution: class and religion. It can be proposed that as no outside aggressor was involved in creating these ruins, the French psyche could do nothing except admit to a French-based culture of ruination and wanton destruction. We can see many religious buildings destroyed by those on both sides, Catholic and Huguenot, and many chateaux decimated by repressed peasants and a dissatisfied *bourgeosie.* Ruins from these times became common currency and a powerful propaganda tool for demoralising the enemy. The Napoleaonic era also brought destruction and privations for the ordinary French person and the revolution of 1848 and the Franco-Prussian War both added to this destruction.

> *"The fact that the emperor had surrendered his sword did not mean that the rest of the country had given up to the enemy. Military and civilian, they fought on with the ferocity of Frenchmen defending their Patrie against the wave after wave of invaders advancing inexorably onto their precious soil."*[2]

Napoleon III, having surrendered, evoked in the French a Gallic determination to continue the fight, a defiant act against their Emperor and Germany which almost cost them their capital, the Siege of Paris being a ruthless attempt by Bismarck and Prussia to break the French spirit through a devastating bombardment of the city and the starving of its citizens.

> "*In almost a complete circle, cannon bearing the ominous name of Krupp were trained on the city*"[3]

The Germans began their bombardment of Paris in the sixteenth week of the siege, one assumes, to further demoralise the citizens with the destruction of their city's buildings. It was starvation though that brought about a capitulation three weeks later. It would take more than the ruination of Paris and the subsequent further destruction caused by the Communards and their civil war devastation, to defeat the French spirit. Perhaps this is a reinforcement of the basis for the French acceptance of its ruined buildings and the collective culture of ruination. They are not afraid of decrepitude and decay after all, as they have faced it so often.

Germany and France had for more than forty years an uneasy truce after the total destruction of France by Germany in the Franco Prussian War of 1871(Fig.1). In 1914, once again these two powers found themselves on the opposite sides in a major conflict, which would be fought mostly on French soil. Germany had a strong determination once again to bombard France into defeat, having been a successful in the Franco-Prussian War. Having said this, all of the combatants had new weapons which could destroy buildings in a moment, so Germany should not shoulder all of the blame for France's ruination. With the development of grenades, flamethrowers and tanks, the obliteration of small communities and large sections of cities was made possible. For instance, the allies used tanks as the major part of a co-ordinated attack alongside artillery and war planes to assist in path clearing for artillery as they pushed forward. This enabled General Monash to achieve a momentous victory at Le Hamel in just 93 minutes, pounding the environment and the army into submission.

The French government's decision to rebuild in 1916, enabled many places devastated by the First World War to be reborn. However, amongst the 3000 villages that it sought to assist in this massive re-development project, there was a large number of villages and their buildings left without funding for restoration. An exposition was held in 1916 where major construction companies in France showed plans for building new villages, a cost of just over $20,000 per settlement. In a report in the New York Times, a clue to the further development of a ruination culture can be found in a comment regarding refugees from the affected areas of France, who attended the *Exposition.*

---

[1] Thomas Mac Greevy., Cron Trath na nDeithe, *Symphonic Poem,* London, 1925

[2] Cornelia Otis Skinner, *Madame Sarah,* London 1966, 70

[3] Cornelia Otis Skinner, *Madame Sarah,* London 1966, 70

Fig. 1 World War I damage

> "*Many of them shed tears at the thought that these new model structures are to take the place of the quaint, irregular buildings that have been associated with their ancestors for generations.*"[1]

As such, many ruined buildings simply were removed or allowed to fall into decay to add to the culture of ruination. Those older buildings left of course, were to face further bombardment in the Second World War. The destruction wrought by the Nazis between 1940-1945 was yet another military, human and cultural violation of a country which had faced ruthless attacks from its old enemy over period of almost a century. It is interesting to note the words in his diary of 1943, of Ernest Junger, a German officer in both wars and a prominent novelist and essayist,

> "*When all buildings shall be destroyed, language will none the less persist. It will be a magic castle with towers and battlements, with primeval vaults and passageways which none will ever search out. There, in deep galleries, oubliettes and mine-shafts it will be possible to find habitation and be lost to the world. Today that thought consoles me.*"[2]

[1] Author unknown, 'France to Rebuild 3000 Ruined Towns', *The New York Times,* 1916, 9

Junger's substitution of language for destroyed buildings systematically draws on the language of ruins themselves, they being so often environments that people do not seek out and equally places of mystery where it is possible to lose oneself. He was a man who had been violently anti-Semitic but who had by the end of the war seen the futility both of what National Socialism stood for and the ultimate pointlessness of its methods which had achieved nothing, as the German army retreated vindictively destroying as much as it could on the way. There was no honour in this retreat, only more devastation, a clear sign of their ethos and its practice having been flawed.

It is interesting to speculate what effect this constant creation of ruination has had on the French psyche; the horror and trepidation of warfare on one's doorstep and the calamity of the bodies of buildings being decimated and exploded. This is something which can perhaps be read also in terms of a damaged human body, and the concomitant fear that that evokes. And yet despite the potential for emotional annihilation, it was the people who went back to their homes and started to rebuild them and their lives. The Germans had destroyed many industries and the very soil of the land so vital to France's economy, and through enforced deportation had also sought to destroy France's culture of the family. It is therefore remarkable how easily and quickly domestic life returned to normal. A pity therefore that not more compensation was made available, but this was impossible for a country brought to its knees in a four year long conflict on its own soil. So, despite the demolition and disappearance and the restoration of many buildings decimated by wars in France, ruinous buildings created by conflicts still are part of the culture of ruination.

Advances in the art of photography and particularly 'war' photography (Fig. 2 First World War damage) and the burgeoning genres of ruination in art and literature as metaphors for deeper human emotions and responses, made it possible to flood the national markets of the major combatants. These are startling depictions of devastation and destruction are expressed in the medium of the *Carte Postale* or Postcards (Fig. 3) (Fig.4), (Fig.5), (Fig.6), (Fig.7), (Fig.8), (Fig.9), (Fig.10). In addition to this, war photography as propoganda reached its apogee during this gruelling conflict. The photographs of ruins, which are still so readily available and collectible, mirrored for a wide audience the technological advances in warfare and the vanity of warring nations. These nations were able to impose crushing and pointless obliteration on each other's cities, towns, and villages. A current thriving business in these '*carte postales*' or postcards of the time, is a testament to the power of ruination occasioned through war, and its iconic status within the movement of ruination, which along a millenia-old spectrum incorporates both ancient and modern buildings alike. These war images are the kind of ruination that one can call 'ruination by design and destruction'. These images are a positive addition to the country's culture of ruination and may continue to assist in the expression of those times through the neglect of buildings now. Depictions of such wanton destruction aroused tremendous emotion in the viewer and this coupled with the historical Romantic view of ruination has been a strong imperative to continue the ruination movement in latter years, despite many of the original wartime ruins having been either bulldozed or rebuilt.

Post Second World War development began almost immediately, but unlike the period after the Great War, involved the massive construction of new modern box-like public rental housing, thereby diverting funding for the restoration of older and damaged properties. Styles change as ever but for the first time public housing became a priority, thereby endangering privately owned old-fashioned buildings. It became a truism that if a person wanted to live in a habitable environment but had limited funds for restoration that the only option was to have a Modernist cube as there was no public monies available for buildings needing compensatory remuneration.

---

[2] Ernest Junger, Prose and Poetry *Prose and Poetry*, 2001 (http://www.firsworldwar.com)

Fig. 2 WWOCP

Fig. 3 (post card)

Fig. 4 WWOCP

Fig. 5 WWOCP

Fig. 6 Word War I damage (post card)

Fig. 7 Word War I damage (post card)

Chapter 4 - The Ruined Chateaux

> *"Like a photograph in the washing, its high lights and shadows come gradually forth. The light splash in the foreground becomes a ruined chateau, the grey street a demolished village."*[1]

As dawn unfolds on another day in the trenches, Alan Seeger (1888-1916) describes the scene before him after a day and night of bombardment. The analogy is appropriate for this photographic monograph, and also draws to mind the wonder when one spots a ruined chateau through a dense wood or over a slowly rising hill in the valley below. Despite being ruined and hidden, many chateaux still maintain the authority they had when they were built and when they were inhabited. They stand defiantly, arrogant, proud and self-assured. They are 'chateaux', and their poise and their never-changing aristocratic bearing comes from that fact. The world knows of their importance, even if current owners treat them with disdain or degrade their status to that of cattle-shed or farm machinery store. So often chateaux are spoken of as great majestic ruins; they have such romance and bear much of France's history on their shoulders, even if their joints and limbs are dilapidated and eroded.

Fig. 1 Chateau Blois - This medieval castle came into royal hands in 1391 when it was bought by Louis, Duc d'Orleans, brother of Charles VI. Other kings who lived their include Louis XII, Francis I, Henri III and Henri IV. The last king to live there was Louis XIII, who gave the castle as a wedding gift to his brother, Gaston Duc d'Orléans.

The word 'Chateau' can be translated as a 'castle' but it is also means 'country house', a manor house or an estate where wine is made and bottled. The word also is used in referring to a royal or noble residence, the chateau at Blois being a good example (Fig. 1).The chateau is often a large and impressive building with an array of outhouses, barns and estate farmhouses (Fig. 2 and Fig. 3). In certain periods, chateaux have fulfilled

[1] William Archer, Poems by Alan Seeger, Part 1 out of 3, on *Fullbooks.com* (http://www.fullbooks.com/Poemsx89491.html; retrieved on the 12th August 2009)

a variety of functions, including a royal or seignurial home and keep in Medieval time, as in England. They would have been bustling places with peasants and serfs taking refuge within their walls during times of conflict. An early secure chateau, called a *château-fort*, the remnants of which can be seen in the re-furbished tower at Chenonceau (Fig 4) reached its apogee in the 1490s to be replaced in the 16th-century by the standardised grand chateau, (Fig. 5) many of which exist today with their gardens, lakes, parkland and other specialised buildings, made either for entertainment or the production of goods. These vast castles, often surrounded by a moat, nevertheless were only fortified lightly. Transitional chateaux between these two distinct periods and styles can be found in the area of Loire Valley and its larger tributaries, the Indre and Cher. This valley, which is home to some 300 of France's many thousands of chateaux, represents architectural splendour spanning a period from the tenth century to the mid twentieth century (Fig. 6. Chateau Le Pin SO). As French kings constructed these edifices to power, the nobility, as it always does, followed suit. The valley is rightly known as the 'Garden of France'.

Fig. 2 Outhouses at Bouges Le Chateau, this small chateau was modeled on the Petit Trianon, private home to Marie Anotinette. Tallyrand, Napoleon's once foreign minister, acquired the house in 1818 and put it at the disposal of his niece Dorothée de Courlande.

Fig. 3 Chateau Le Pin, farm

The Revolution of 1789 witnessed a number of the great French chateaux being destroyed and many ransacked, their treasures stolen. The deposing of the chateau owning nobility caused many chateaux to be demolished. Of the many chateaux remaining, some are privately owned homes, (Fig 7) with some being at the centre of the Tourist trade as visitor centres (Fig. 8). Also local government authorities sometimes have taken over large chateaux and they have become major tourist sites, feeding the romantic desires and historical communities of many people across the world.

Fig. 4 Chateau Chenonceau - This chateau owes its existence and development to women. Being built by Katherine Briconnet in 1513, enriched by Diane de Poitiers (mistress of Henri II) and Catherine de Medici (wife of Henri II) and saved during the French Revolution by Madame Dupin.

Fig. 5 Chateau Valencay - The chateau was once owned by the notorious Scottish banker and economist John Law. Half a century later Napoleon ordered his foreign minister to buy the property as a gilded prison for Ferdinand VII of Spain, who spent six years there. During the Second World War and as the Tallyrand-Perigord family had nominal control of the Duchy of Sagan in Prussian Silesia, the then owner of Valencay, the Duke of Sagan, having checked his neutrality, offered his home as a safe and neutral place for treasures from the Louvre to be safely housed including the 'Venus de Milo'.

Fig. 6. Chateau Le Pin

Fig 7 Chateau near Valencay

Fig. 8 Chateau d'Amboise - This marvelous building in the 15th century became a favourite of French kings. The castle was extensively rebuilt by Charles VIII in the late 15th century and in 1515 Leonardo da Vinci came to live in the area and work on the chateau under the watchful eye of Francis I. Mary Queen of Scots was raised in the castle along with the children of Henri II and Catherine de Medici.

Fig. 9 Chateau de Valencay

When one thinks of places of interest in France for tourist and artist alike, the mind is always drawn to the Chateaux. Every place large or small, has a chateau, some in pristine condition and some in a parlous state (Fig. 9, Fig. 10). They exist in various shapes and sizes also (Fig. 11 and Fig. 13).

These buildings form a large proportion of the total ruined buildings in France and sit easily within the *oeuvre* of Romanticism that has found expression within and beyond France. Even today 'the chateaux' epitomise France as much as wine or cheese. These symbols signify the country like nothing else.

Fig. 10 Chateau le Lude - Some famous visitors include Henry IV, Louis XIII (father of Louis XIV, The Sun King) and Marquise de Sévigné, a French aristocrat, noted for her published letter writing.

Fig. 11 Chateau de Rothschild

Fig. 12 Chateau de Bressuire

Fig. 13 Chateau Tours D'Aigues

As symbols of the corrupt aristocracy of pre-revolutionary France, chateaux were always going to be vulnerable to destruction by a discontented bourgouisie and peasantry (Fig. 12), a dereliction which has continued through the intervening years of subsequent revolutions and wars. Also, as elsewhere in the world, such buildings require an enormous amount of money to maintain. Taking these considerations into account, what follows is a selection of ruined chateaux of varying degrees of size and importance with short descriptions for each.

1. Chateau Soulges, (Fig. 14)

This place is a small and rambling complex, now fully restored after years of neglect. A typical example of a French house where it is difficult to tell whether it is inhabited or not, as its appearance could simply belie either a working farm or a closed up deserted ruin.

2. Chateau de la Mothe, (Fig. 15 & 16)

The castle of Mothe-Chandeniers had always been owned by the family Hennecart Lorsqu. At the time of its last habitation before it burned down in 1932, the proprietor had an enthusiasm for horse racing. It was whilst attending such an event with his mother that a fire broke out in the chateau, which the local community despite rallying to the needs of the chateau, could not extinguish. The crowds looked on helplessly as the fire raged leaving only a habitable vault at the rear of the castle, which still exists today. The chateau is a ruin, despite having the effect of tricking the viewer into believing it is still a magical and traditional French castle, alive to the machinations of humans.

3. Chateau Tours d'Aigues, (Fig. 17)

This 16th century chateau having been partly damaged by fire in 1780 was nine years later a victim of a French Revolutionary mob, which ransacked the building, plundered its treasures and set light to it. Its owner, Baron Jean-Baptiste-Jerome de Bruny, was luckily absent. Despite the castle taking five days to burn down, it is probable, given the history of lawsuits between the Baron and the local community, that much stored up resentment was expunged during this event, as in other parts of France during the Revolution. The building, which slipped into ruination in the ensuing century and became a place of reclamation for the villagers, was bought by the local government in 1897, which enabled the safe keeping of the fine ruin one sees today. The crisp lines of this fabulous chateau are delineated to great effect against the sky.

4. Chateau Varennes, (Figs. 18, 19, 20)
A middle sized chateau, dated 1570 and re-built for Francois of the Vault, now re-roofed and yet an empty shell. An interesting interior feature is the revealed vaulting between floors. The chateau was attacked and devastated at the end of the religious wars. In 1688, the castle was completely abandoned by its new Masters. The chateau in these pictures looks devoid of life, despite on the surface appearing to be a complete building.

5. Chateau de la Tour, Folleville (Fig. 21)
Folleville was built in fourteenth century and it dominates its landscape and the valley which it overlooks. Already in the early 17th century, the Count de Mailly decided to use the stones of this imposing castle to rebuild another chateau in Mailly-Raineval. Today, vestiges of the castle of Folleville, its machicolations and waste-gas mains can be seen by visiting the site.

6. Chateau de Valencay (Fig. 22)

A small outbuilding situated at an entrance to the gardens of this fabulous chateau, once the home of Napoleon's foreign minister, Tallyrand. It is seen here in the process of refurbishment following the local commune taking over the running of the chateau once again. It has the look of a house and may have been a grace and favour apartment for a member of staff. As with other out-buildings of the chateau estate, this one is benefitting from a surge of restoration, which includes the chateau itself.

7. Chateau de Crozant (Fig. 23)

A popular tourist spot, the castle dominates a bend in the valley of the Creuse river. The ruins of the citadel cover much of the spur, with a tower from the fifteenth century and two towers of the thirteenth, also a small chapel and the ingenious "water tower" which allowed people to 'fetch water from the river while staying covered from rain, snow or stray arrows'.

8. Chateau Chauvigny (Fig. 24)
A stark ruin, home to a community of eagles, set high on a hillside overlooking the town. The chateau is actually five chateaux in one; the Bishop's Chateau, the Chateau D'Harcourt, the Chateau de Montleon, The Gouzon dungeon and the Tours de Flins. The fact that it is composed of a variety of separate buildings explains its odd silhouette. It was abandoned and used as stone quarry.

9. Chateau de Rothschild, Paris (Fig. 25, 26, 27, 28, 29)

This is a massive cosmopolitan chateau on the West side of Paris - a rarity indeed in such a large city. The Rothschild family's once-grand chateau is in ruins. It is incredulous that this fine building has been allowed to deteriorate, rather than it being saved for the nation, using the house in some civic or entertainment role or else completely tearing it down. No doubt some ancient French property law, bureaucratic issues or, as in many cases, complex inheritance squabbles have resulted in the current situation, although its size may have prohibited its restoration. The family donated the park and the surrounding land - which is prime real estate due to its position directly opposite the Bois du Boulogne - to the city. Discussions proceed as ever into the future of the charming grand chateau, and it is hoped that some solution is found before the constantly sinking chateau dissolves into a mass of rubble. Ugly tarpaulins and graffiti mark this out as a major urban ruin.

10. Chateau du Lude (Fig. 30, 31, 32, 33)
The original fort built around the tenth to eleventh centuries was remodelled into a charming palace in the late 1400's and continued to be embellished for over two centuries. This once impressive gatehouse is now falling into decay despite the main chateau building being a lively tourist venue.

11. Chateau Villentrois (Fig. 34, 35, 36)
A selection of photos of buildings in the village of Villentrois, including the fort-feudal or chateau and remnants of various estate buildings. The fort was built between twelfth to fifteenth centuries and has had protected status since 1925.

12. Chateau de Bressuire (Fig. 37, 38)

There has been a building on this site since Celtic times. The building which one can now see ruined was built between the tenth and eleventh centuries by the Beaumont family. The building dominates a rounded upland and this strong position was crucial during the battles of Poitou fought between the English and the French. It remained in the Beaumont-Bressuire family until the start of the sixteenth century. The new chateau to be glimpsed sitting further back from the ruins dates from the late eighteenth century. The Commune has owned the chateau since 1975.

13. Chateau Le Pin (Figs. 39 - 54)

The chateau was last lived in the mid 1970's and is now an empty shell with part of the rear elevation wall collapsed. It is surrounded by dense forest and only reveals itself in the Autumn/Winter as the leaves fall. Inner floors have disappeared, and the roof in places is overhanging precariously, and a tower has become a home to a silver birch tree. During the time of writing this book, nature has overtaken the house in a spectacular fashion, the interior now a home to many large sapling trees and almost impenetrable as a result.

14. Chateau Villedieu (Figs. 55-65)
Former Fort-Feudal now a golf club and a dramatic ruin, of the Seventeenth century.

15. Chateau Sandillon (Fig. 66)

This is a well manicured ruin, close to Orléans.

16. Chateau Bijou (Figs. 67-77)

Originally an eighteenth century country house designed by Dussine. It was completely transformed at the beginning of the twentieth century by Mrs Combes, née Saint-Macary, who lavished spectacular sums of money on building the new chateau. The building you see today, although much devastated through fire and also through neglect, with its stucco bas-reliefs, cornices and coloured frescoes, still entrances the viewer. The main highlights are the Neo-Gothic chapel and a cloister reassembled with columns and capitals from the Medieval period in a Hispano-Franco style. The French police mutual insurance company, former owners of the chateau before it was recently purchased by a private buyer, allowed its subscribers to stay in the chateau for holidays. It had in recent times though been abandoned especially after a fire, which occasioned the application of an ugly tin roof. The park, chapel, gardens, ornamental lake and water reservoir have only been listed as historical monuments since 2005 and much work must be undertaken to restore this dynamic and rare twentieth century gem to its true magnificence. The whole complex has an air of faded Art Deco glamour or of an old film set mansion, the kind in which Norma Desmond lived, in the film 'Sunset Boulevard'.

17. Chateau de Bidache, (Fig. 78, 79)

The medieval castle which was destroyed in 1523 reveals only three round towers now. The castle after this devastation was transformed by Renaissance architects, whilst maintaining a protective infrastructure. The celebrated seventeenth century architect Louis de Mihet was then given the task of modernising this estate by adding gardens and terraces, and in the Eighteenth century a vast pedimented doorway was added before the whole estate was confiscated for the Nation during the Revolution in 1793. A brief reprieve was given to the complex shortly afterwards when a military hospital was set up there before a fire devastated the whole place in 1796. This is a truly magnificent edifice standing alone. The chateau was owned by the Gramont family. The most famous member of this family was Anotine III de Gramont, who was married to the niece of Cardinal Richelieu and was a friend of Cardinal Mazarin.

18. Castle Uhar Mixe (Fig. 80-83)
The fifteenth to eighteenth century castle of Uhar Mixe on the road between Saint Palais and Saint Jean Pied de Port in the Basque country. It was owned by an aristocrat in the 1950's, who was the last person to live there. After he sold the house, a priest converted it into a holiday home for under-privileged children. It may be in line to be renovated by a Frenchman. This building bears the marks of neglect, clearly a slow progression, as many beautiful details remain, despite being spoiled and faded.

STRVCTA CLEMETIS
D'VHARTIS ET MARCARITÆ DE MONEINS
CVRA ANNO 1699

19. Chateau de Bearn-Sendos (Fig. 84 & 85)

A castle with amazing architecture of the sixteenth century, which replaced a feudal mound of which "The Baque gentil", a local pre-Christian people, were lords. The primitive castle was on the boundary between the

lands of the Kings of England and those of the Viscount of Béarn during the One Hundred Years War. The castle has been in disuse as a home since 1945 and is now used as an agricultural store.

21. Chateau de Caresse Casabar (Fig. 86 & 87)

This house is left to decay despite having been bought by people from the Netherlands. A romantic image as nature seems to be taking control of this building once again. It is a typical three story country house.

Here a collection of ruined chateaux has been discussed and displayed, an impressive cross-section of architectural periods and styles, all buildings with a chequered past and interesting stories attached to them. This chapter has served to reinforce the assertion that ruins have been a part of life in France as in other countries for millennia, and will probably continue to be so in the future. The culture of ruin is a strong one and the French still seem to have ambivalent feelings towards the ruined buildings themselves, sometime spilling over into an exuberant defence of a building when it is threatened but unwilling to halt the process by which a building can come to the brink of such destruction. As with domestic buildings, many fixtures and fittings in a chateaux can and do feed the booming reclamation market in a way that industrial and religious buildings do not. Once a piece of machinery has seized up and rusted it is unlikely to fetch a price at re-sale but a paint stripped medieval panel or a grand fireplace from a chateau can fetch enormous prices and sometimes its state of decay can work even more in its favour as some people seek the 'distressed aged look' more than the new. Perhaps this is also indicative of the general acceptance of things beautiful even if they are perished in some way.

Chapter 5 - Ruined and Deserted Domestic Buildings

> *"Each of us is a ruined house. Each of us pays the penalty of death. These strange words echo from somewhere in the depths of my being, and I quietly listen and write them down. I often feel overwhelmed by the ruin of my own life."*[1]

Domestic buildings take many forms, the chateaux of France, discussed in the previous chapter, being but one variety. Chateaux have filled, and continue to fulfill, a public role at the centre of local communities, and as solid and large-scale producers of revenue for the local and national economy. Alternatively, smaller domestic buildings serve the owners and their families.

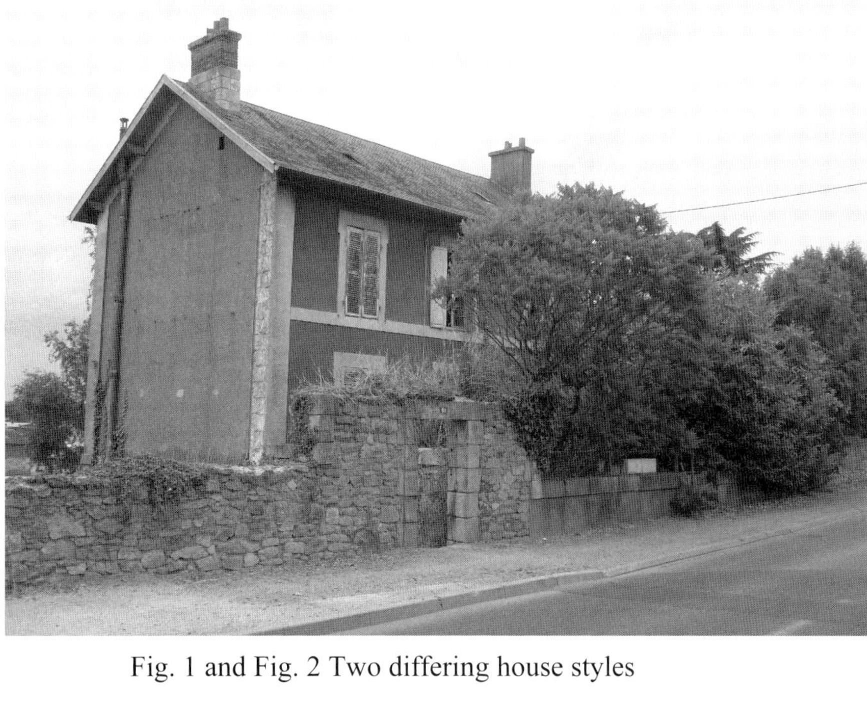

Fig. 1 and Fig. 2 Two differing house styles

[1] Sitaram, *The Owl in a Ruined House*, 2004 (http://www.online-literature.com/forums/showthread.php?t=13276, retrieved November 2009)

These smaller domestic establishments have numerous design types although often Departments or Regions have a distinct overall pattern; the Indre and Gironde are seen here (Fig. 1 and Fig. 2). For the purposes of this chapter, 'domestic' includes houses, (Fig. 3), outbuildings (Fig. 4) barns, (Fig. 5) small workshops and stores attached to houses. People may find it incredulous to see a ruined house, but it is perhaps less surprising to see ruined outbuildings or barns as these are generally not for human habitation. Changes in the economy or the unwanted bequest of a house with many other buildings attached can prohibit the maintenance of an older property and its outbuildings. (Fig. 6)

Fig. 3 House Cormery

Fig. 4 Outbuilding Chateau Le Pin Farm

Fig. 5 Barns, Corroir de Fez

Fig. 6 Older property, Levroux

It is part of human nature to anthropomorphise objects, and ruined buildings are no exception to this pattern in human psychology and the overwhelming imperative in people to impose a story on 'things'. We have seen in Balzac's *Le Grande Breteche*, the way in which the main character talks of a ruined building with passion and with a sense of forbidden fruit, he longs to return to commune with the mysterious house with the dilapidated gardens and the walls, overgrown with ivy. Houses large or small can fall prey to such attribution of hominid characteristics by the spectator. As small houses are by their nature more personal and private, (Fig. 7) it is perhaps a little easier to romanticise about the individuals who may have lived in them and about the details of how a building has come to be deserted, neglected and ruined.

Fig. 7 Aunt Alphonisne's house, La Maison Mère

Of course, smaller ruins have benefited precisely *because of* their size, making them easier and cheaper to renovate. It is possible to see all over France an explosion of restoration projects usually on houses of lesser proportions, and yet the countryside is still littered with the smaller ruin, buildings held in contempt often as being over simple and unworthy of notice. The Gallic shrug of dismissal for a ruined building, which has allowed so many ruins to escape the bulldozer, is neatly counter-balanced by the calculated desire of foreigners, particularly the British, to restore the quaint old buildings of France to a kind of former glory, not always successfully. Non-French restorers can quite naturally slip into turning a French country cottage into an English one. The ex-pat revolution in restoration has most often occurred at this domestic level of ruination, where it can be easier to create a new and often transformed building out of an old derelict shell. To try to do that to a Chateau de La Mothe Fig. 25 Chapter 4 or a Grand Hotel de Salies Bearn Fig. 51 Chapter 7 is inconceivable. These places are iconic and far too immense to be overly reconstructed; they also can carry historic monument status which very few smaller domestic buildings will have.

Examples of domestic ruins abound and here are just a few displaying the variety to be found throughout France.

1. La Maison Mère (Fig. 8 & 9)

A small house attached to another house belonging to a neighbour. This house was last inhabited in the late 1950's by the current owner's late Great aunt Alphonsine. The house is part of a larger compound with a large house, attached outbuildings and barn opposite. The little house has always been surplus to requirements and would be a potential drain on resources if it were to be restored and maintained, The front corner of the house is collapsing as is the rear elevation roof. Even the large house is generally uninhabited apart from occasional visitors.

2. Couffy (Fig. 10)

A small house once attached to the one owned by the author. It has an air of mystery about it as local mythology is that it used to be a postal service staging post as it has a grand dormer window, dated 1888. It is slowly and mercilessly being overtaken by nature as the current owner once again does not have the desire or finance to restore it. It had a grand dormer window but this was blown out in a recent storm and now lies in a pile by the front door. In December 2010, this house was completely demolished.

3. Lye (Figs. 11 & 12)
A small house, part of a farm complex, roofless and almost totally overgrown with vines and brambles, the roof timbers acting as a kind of fretwork pergola for nature. Opposite this building is a working farm.

4. Couffy town (Fig. 13)

A small house on the main street in front of a small commercial premises. Locked up by both padlocks and a closely-knit covering of ivy. A thriving commercial unit can be found at its rear.

5. Chabris (Fig. 14)

This is a small barn next to a single farmhouse. Its skeletal network form is particularly attractive at sunset.

6. Paizay Le Sec (Figs. 15 & 16)
A quite large farmhouse on the main street, deserted and falling into dis-repair. The roof tiles having slipped and a hole having formed means the death knell for this charming house is sounding.

7. Maisoncelle (Fig. 17 & 18)
A medium sized house, overgrown with vegetation and with a large complex of outbuildings, all deserted and usused. Once again nature is taking hold of this human edifice.

8. Close to Le Lude (Figs. 19 - 22)
A tiny roadside house with a distinct style of ruination to be seen its roof redolent of draped fabric. It is interesting to see a once rigid structure behaving like nature itself.

9. Mirabeau (Fig. 23)
A small house set in amongst modernised buildings and yet falling down and dilapidated, right in the middle of a large village.

10. Bressuire (Fig. 24)
Bressuire is a small town house in the heart of this town, locked up and neglected.

11. Close to Le Lude (Figs. 25 - 30)
Two ruined and deserted roadside buildings.

12. Entraigues (Fig. 31)
A fairy-tale farmhouse perched on a small hill not far from a stunning chateau. It is in the shadow of a great tree which is slowly taking it over from above and presumably from below.

13. Chateau Le Pin farm (Fig. 32)
This ruined farm complex on an estate of a spectacular ruined shell of a once impressive chateau. It has a farmhouse, attached barns and store houses all in a vast L-shape, and all in a parlous state. Some renovation work has been begun, but maybe this is too large a project for anyone. It also has two towers nearby the use of which is unknown, although they do seem to form an entrance which may lead across to the ruined chateau in the woods.

14. Le Lude (Fig. 33)
A small house within the walls of the chateau and close to the deserted and decaying gate house.

15. Close to Le Lude (Figs. 34 & 35)
A small farm with outbuildings, rear elevation close to and facing the road.

6. Dinan (Fig. 36 & 37)

A large building, boarded up and deserted, surrounded by similar buildings in varying stages of renovation.

17. Scorbie-Clarivaux (Fig. 38 - 42)

A large town house now inherited by two individuals who are finding it difficult to agree on what to do with the building. The building is open to the elements and in danger of irreversible damage as a result.

18. Pellevoisin (Fig. 43 & 44)
A small farmhouse with outbuildings close to the road, left to fall into ruin.

19. St. Martin De Lamps (Fig. 45)
Another small farmhouse complex, now surrounded by farmland with no visible means of access.

20. Fez (Figs. 46 - 49)
A medium sized farm complex visible and standing at a crossroads. The house is falling into disrepair and one outbuilding collapsing, revealing an intricate network of roofing supports.

21. Farm near Valencay (Fig. 50)

22. Hidden farm building near Valencay (Fig. 51)

This complex is overgrown with vegetation and almost completely hidden from the road.

23. Vierzon (Fig. 52)

A large timber framed house by the canal. There is evidence of an attempt at restoration but all is quiet now.

24 .Vierzon (Fig. 53 & 54)
A gap between two houses in the old quarter of Vierzon. It is not clear what happened to initiate this ruined shell, with stove flues and even wallpaper still visible.

25. Caresse Casabar (Figs. 55 -59)
A medium sized house now ruined and derelict abutting a new housing development built on the house's former gardens. The house was bought as part of the development but the Historic Monuments authority rejected the demolition application. The house is now being left to decay and to be overrun by vines and long grasses, to justify its future demolition.

* * *

It is perhaps more difficult to categorise domestic ruined and deserted buildings, as they most often do not have epic battles, struggles or events at the root of their destruction. They can be so often the victims of financial or legal battles that can so afflict the ordinary man and woman, but they can so easily be dismissed out of hand as being of no historical importance. Therefore they can slip into decrepitude with startling ease and that is why the French countryside is littered with them, the examples given here being only a small portion of the total. In human and sociological terms though they are as important as the biggest and grandest chateau or abbey, and locate themselves equally firmly in the nation's psyche and cultural life.

Chapter 6 - Ruined Religious Buildings

> *"No more the cowl or rosary known; The Monkish garb and worship are no more;*
> *Those walls are moulder'd where the list'ning stone Heard Superstition frame its solemn roar"*[1]

Ruined religious buildings abound globally, from pagan temples through to Christian monuments and beyond. France's diverse cultural heritage includes religious buildings such as monasteries, (Fig. 1) *abbayes*, (Fig. 2) cathedrals, (Fig. 3) churches (Fig. 4) and chapels (Fig. 5).

Fig.1 Chateau convent close to Loches

Fig. 2 Bourges

[1] Joseph Jefferson, *The Ruins of a Temple,* London, 1793

Fig. 3 Abbaye de Cormery

Fig. 4 Romorantin

Fig. 5 Valencay Chapel

There are many abbayes in France and some of the best examples date from the Eleventh and Twelfth centuries and include Senanque, Silvacane, Fontenay and Pontingny and some lesser ones such as the one at Loches (Fig.6 & 7). Cathedrals, the seat of bishops, are many in France and the Gothic culture is best exemplified in the cathedrals of Chartres, Reims and Paris, Notre-Dame (Fig.8). Alternatively Poitiers (Fig.9) with its original painted columns is a pure expression of the Romanesque style, whilst Saint-Denis and Lourdes are known as basilica churches.

Fig. 6 Abbaye de Loches - The resting place of Agnes Sorel, mistress of Charles VII of France, whose chateau sits beside the church, a gift of her royal lover and also the scene of his meeting with Joan of Arc, who persuaded him to be crowned king of France.

Fig. 7 Abbaye de Loches

Fig. 8 Notre Dame de Paris - Various royal events have taken place in this church including the coronations of Henry VI of England as King of France and of Napoleon Bonaparte as Emperor, the marriages of Mary, Queen of Scots and the Dauphin Francis and that of Henri IV and Marguerite de Valois and the Requiem Mass for General de Gaulle.

Fig. 9 - Poitiers Cathedral, Construction of this marvellous Romanesque and early Gothic cathedral was begun by Henry II of England and his wife Eleanor of Aquitaine.

One of the most popular religious buildings of France is the Notre Dame de Paris, dedicated to the Virgin Mary. A major tourist attraction and one of the finest examples of French Gothic architecture. (Fig. 10 & Fig. 11)

Fig. 10 & Fig. 11 Notre Dame de Paris

We have already noted that some buildings were destroyed during the Revolution of 1789, often by angry mobs, thereby creating ruins. Often however religious buildings suffered because their communities of monks, abbots and priests were expelled and afterwards a larger parish or community could not find a use for the building. This can be seen at the Abbey of Notre Dame du Lys and the Abbaye de Cormery, (Fig.12) both of which were allowed to fall into decrepitude, although they are now cleaned up and are spectacular ruins.

Fig. 12 Abbaye de Cormery

Many churches were also targeted during wars, particularly the Great War (1914-18) and the Second World War, such as the church at Oradour, which was used as a death-trap for innocent women and children. As an important component of French culture and spiritual support, religious buildings were the obvious target for enemy fire. However, the intent to dishearten often rallied the peoples of France and other countries into a steely determination to overcome adversity, and in the case of Oradour to create a sublime and deeply moving memorial. Ruins, particularly those of churches, have been turned into cultural and memorial icons of a national strength of character.
Religious buildings are always built to last but it is well documented that the ongoing maintenance and cost of that upkeep is large, indeed often prohibitive. With large-scale buildings such as churches and cathedrals commanding immeasurable amounts of money for Conservation projects due in part to their historical and cultural importance, it is no wonder that many fall into disrepair, with the best they can hope for being a stripping of their roofs and other

timbers and removal of stained or other glass, thereby creating the classic *'touristique'* model of ruin. The very size of religious buildings creates its own problems.

Religious house of Corrorerie (Fig. 13). A Medieval Carthusian monastery situated in the forest of Loches. Now a well kept ruin and tourist destination and place to stay. The whole complex is completed by a lake opposite, which often sends a swirling mist over the hamlet.

Beaucamp Seminary (Fig. 14 & 15)
Beaucamp Seminary was developed by the Marist brothers and closed down due to religious intolerance in 1904. The ruins of the old seminary are seen to be overgrown and derelict in the photograph.

One of the author's antecedents studied there at the seminary. The other image is an impressive early drawing of the complete seminary.

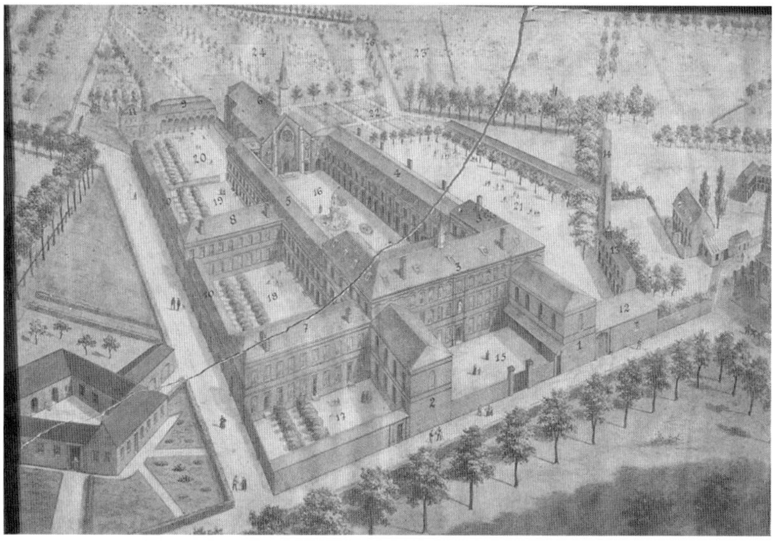

3. La Cropte (Fig. 16)
A small Norman chapel which now forms part of the garden of the *Mairie*.

4. L'abbaye Notre-Dame du Landais (Fig. 17 & 18)
A formerly large twelfth century religious house, built around a cloistered courtyard and following the French Revolution and progressively broken up for the construction of other buildings in the locality. There is only one corner of the religious building remaining. The barn which runs parallel to the road once housed a Renaissance portal destroyed only as recently as 1960.

5. Uridos Chapel (Fig. 19 & 20)
A small unused eleventh and twelfth century chapel, used now as a farm outbuilding, with access to outsiders denied.

* * *

Often religious ruined buildings have been saved for posterity, perhaps as a mark of national respect and pride. However, it is often the small abandoned churches, chapels or remnant of a larger establishment that have a purer appeal. Small, unimportant and rejected by communities and private owners, they often evoke a deeper spiritual aura, better than many larger ruins given over to tourism and the imperative for profit, which feeds the on-going maintenance of these great edifices.

Chapter 7 - Ruined and Deserted Civic Buildings and Commercial Buildings

> "*They are matter out of place, a continuing rebuke to attempts to render urban space productive, smooth and regular.* "[1]

Civic and commercial buildings in France are as varied as in any other major developed country. They are supremely functional of course, a truly French requirement and yet also beautiful, fascinating, modern for the buildings' time and innovative. The following are examples of some civic and commercial buildings:Farm buildings for a whole commune, (Fig.1) water mills, fairly recently deserted industrial units (Fig.2), beautifully proportioned railway buildings (Fig.3), garages and shops. The imperative for ruination in commercial buildings can be different to that found in domestic buildings. These commercial premises may outlive their profitability and not be suitable for alteration to another commercial or domestic use. Alternatively they can be victims of an economic downturn as an area changes its economic base, as in the case of a hotel in Valencay, now sharply contrasting with the beautifully refurbished station (Fig.4).

Fig.1 Vatan

It is not difficult to understand why some civic buildings become ruins. Schools close down in the wake of developments in educational techniques or political ideology. Railway stations, rather like those in an England of the 1960's, are closed down as transport becomes more centralised and urban centre focussed. All of this a sign of the ever-changing times in which we live.

[1] Tim Edensor, *British Industrial Ruins*, *(http://images.wikia.com/abaete/images/b/b6/Journal_Material_Culture_10(3).pdf)*

Fig. 2 Valencay   Fig. 3 Le Blanc

Fig. 4 Abandoned and decaying hotel in Valencay

Fig. 5 A railway shed

Now, ruined commercial buildings can have a new lease of life whilst still being ruins. Many ruined commercial buildings have been and could be in the future, utilised as a space for a piece of avant-garde performance art, a concert, a film set or a photo shoot; even 'Vogue' magazine used burnt out ruins in Post War fashion shoots, juxtaposing *haute couture* with derelict and faded mansions or factories. The two examples here express the diversity of ruined and deserted commercial buildings (Fig.5 & Fig. 6).

Fig. 6 A cinema

What is the process of ruination in civic and commercial buildings? Rather like in other domestic and religious buildings in fact. The processes of ruination can be similar for all ruined environments. The more perishable of building materials and interior fittings will go first, although in fact if a building is left long enough with its roof, windows and doors intact, an interior can last for a very long time. So, aside from the building itself which may or may not erode quicker than say a château or barn, we can see within civic or commercial buildings there is more of a tendency to have permanent fixtures: drilling machines, water pumps, sluice gates, blackboards, lockers and ticket machines. Most of these, being made of metal or enclosed in metal, will last longer than a plaster cornice or a wooden stable. Taking an old water mill as an example: First the metal machinery may seize up from disuse. At the same time any water that remains may now be standing still creating damp conditions, which in turn will speed up the process in which the building, housing all this machinery, is overtaken by the forces of nature. The metal, after a period, will also begin to rust and paint will begin to strip away. Timbers in doors, windows, and the roof may also begin to rot and over time collapse, allowing further moisture and bad weather to permeate the building's fabric, taking the building to the next level of ruination and decay. As more fragile parts of the infrastructure collapse, the building will take on a new shape and the holes made initially through the weakness of wood will become bigger and allow the cycle of rusting inside the building to continue, stone or concrete may become weakened by the loss of the wooden components, and begin to fail. Also, if the mill is in an urban setting then the other threat to it may already have been vandalism. Some civic and commercial buildings are discussed here:

1. St.Aignan School (Fig. 7, 8, 9)
An empty and deserted school, with large arched entrance. A massive complex probably once a boarding school. A grand building sadly neglected and ripe for alternative use. There is a series of farm buildings surrounding the complex.

2. Roscoff (Fig. 10)
A former military building now devoid of glass and timber or metal framing revealing only the concrete infrastructure. Nature is taking back this premises.

3. Cormery (Fig. 11)
A folly 'Villa Marguerite' close to the old station, a miniature building reminiscent of a dolls house.

4. Watermill Cormery (Fig. 12)
A giant former watermill in the centre of Cormery, now devoid of roof and wooden window frames. Set amongst a vibrant residential community and close to the nearby Abbaye de Cormery.

5. Cormery (Fig. 13)
A small building probably devoted to light industry close to the old station. Now it is totally covered with ivy.

6. Orthez (Fig. 14)
A grand tower, a remnant of a much larger former civic building in Orthez.

7. Le Blanc (Fig. 15, 16, 17)
Two buildings in a complex including the old station, currently being renovated. The building you see with the graffiti is what can be called a clean ruin, well cared for devoid of fittings, which have all been removed and with only a limited incursion of nature.

8. Levroux (Fig. 18, 19, 20, 21, 22, 23, 24)
A range of industrial units closely situated to the north of this town. They seem to form a 'ghetto' of mainly wood based constructions now standing empty and dilapidated.

9. Reuilly (Fig. 25 & 26)
A workshop in ruins with an attached wooden building, its walls collapsing.

10. Reuilly (Fig. 27)
Small building unused and with an enormous crack running down its front elevation.

11. Reuilly (Fig. 28, 29, 30)
A redundant *Cafe des Sports* on the way out of the village. The open secondary glazing on one door afforded the picture of the sad interior.

12. Moulin (Fig. 31)
A now defunct commercial grain store just outside Reuilly.

13. Bourges (Fig. 32)
A small commercial building set within a thriving commercial neighbourhood packed with small businesses.

14. Near to Dreux (Fig. 33)
A deserted garage

15. Grand Hotel de France, Salies de Bearn (Fig. 34, 35, 36, 37, 38, 39)

Grand Hotel de France et d'Angleterre partly destroyed by fire in 1998, although the shell seems sound. There have been some plans to turn the facade and building into an exclusive spa, as yet not implemented. The heavy maintenance requirements and costs of upgrading - estimated at more than ten million francs is prohibitive for the current owner.

The hotel is not listed or registered, but has a hundred component parts, including fifty rooms on five levels with a 4 800 m2 covered terrace facing the south and beautiful architecture of the nineteenth century. Salies de Bearn was a major in the late nineteenth and earlytwentieth centuries and the privileged classes flocked to its Moorish inspired spa.

* * *

Commercial properties are often at the greatest risk of being deserted and falling into ruination. They not only rely on their owners, but they have to withstand the topsy-turvy world of commerce, the ever changing financial markets both local and national. Maybe for this reason what we see more than anywhere else is the wanton dispassionate desertion of buildings and their fixtures and fittings, and even in some cases their products. Yet they too, as other ruins, chronicle a nation's past achievements, downturns and cultural design. A new interest and discipline has developed over the last two hundred years as the Industrial Revolution with its vast factories and warehouses became the latest in a long line of styles of buildings to fall victim to the ruination process. Many of the commercial buildings here are recent ruins but no doubt France and the French, as elsewhere, have seen ruined commercial and industrial buildings since the early nineteenth century.

Chapter 8 - The Psychology of Ruination

> "*Yet ruins survive. They are an intermediate stage between creation and destruction, affording, Janus-like, a view into the past and the future; existing in both present and past, without belonging to either; displaying the marks of the teeth of time, and enduring in stimulative physicality. Neither survival nor death can surround them; they present a third existence, living virus-like only in the minds of the beholder. Ruins are the exiles of time.*"[1]

Ruins can be a way for the human psyche to deal with the loss and decay that each of us faces. They can be exemplars for the many minor and major deaths that every human faces in their lives, as people leave us, ideas and plans change for us, as our bodies and minds fail and dependence looms. They can remind us of a pleasant place and the dreadful event which may have transformed our view of that place. Ruins at the same time being uninhabitable are safe emotional spaces that we do not have to embed ourselves in, that thing that changed for us does not, nay cannot, happen there again, because we are not able to be there all of the time; no one is. Therefore our injured psyche and mental and physical breakdown are, in some way perhaps, supported by the 'ruin'. Ruins are therefore a safe space to deal with our psychological hurts and the vicissitudes of life. They are exiles from reality as well as time, safe spaces that have no future and no past, only a present of continuing dereliction.

> "*Nothing forces us, however, to envisage the becoming-cyborg of humanity as the shipwreck of civilization. More generally, it may very well be that the anxious character of many contemporary landscapes is the indication of profound transformations affecting the definition of the subject who contemplates them, without such transformations necessarily being synonymous with the irremediable degradation of the human condition.*"[2]

Antoine Picon is clearly talking of modern designed landscapes here, those created out of *nothing,* where before there was *nothing*. However, his assertion can also apply to ruined landscapes, born as they are out of a *no-thingness* or an *absence* of care or actual attendance. (Fig. 1)

Fig. 1 Near Le Lude

---

[1] *Dr. Michael Haldane's Translation Homepage, Internet pages,* 2009 (http://michaelhaldane.com/Translation%20and%20Ruin%20Ch.%201.htm)

[2] *Antoine Picon,, translated by Karen Bates,Anxious Landscapes: From the Ruin to Rust, 2009* (http://www.gsd.harvard.edu/people/faculty/picon/ruinerouille.pdf)

Another important psychological aspect to a ruin can be a 'running away', a flight from a difficult or shocking situation or collective human shame about an incident, expressed most effectively at the village of Oradour, where following a Nazi atrocity involving the murder of hundreds of French civilians. General Charles de Gaulle of France decided that the village would never be rebuilt. Instead, it would remain as a memorial to and a symbol of the cruelty of the Nazi occupation. Another example can be found at Celles where a whole village was abandoned after a shocking flood occurred during the construction of a dam.

Fig. 2 Near Le Lude

It is clear also that not only our darker emotions but our romantic natures are stirred by ruined buildings. Romance and sentiment are a strong part of the psychology of the human being. Ruins fulfill a role as 'performative structures' of 'love and no-love'; we need only think of the main character in Balzac's, *La Grande Breteche,* to recognise the cause of the ruination of the house he so admires. This is the ever present dichotomy for us of 'belonging and not belonging', experienced along the frequency of human subjectivity, as opposed to the objective action experienced by us as witnessed by Foucault's 'normal and abnormal', mentioned in an earlier chapter to explain another aspect of ruins. This aspect is that of a dissident force, at once a normal result of desertion, itself a dissident act for many, and a defiant and deviant act by the building in refusing to disappear or to be allowed to disappear. (Fig. 2)

> *"There are significant parallels that exist in the co-constitutive relationship between ruin and self, between broken space and broken psyche. The interpretive act of reading ruin is a geographical inquiry that can lend itself to a process of autobiographical imagination, where the ruin seeker takes in the environment, initially observing ethnographically to eventually understand introspectively. As Robert Harbison notes, "ruins are such a glaring example of architecture existing largely in the mind, or in the eye of the beholder. . . . one can say they are just a way of seeing or a state of soul" (10). A site of imaginative production, ruin positions the inquisitive spectator as imaginer with a*

reflective/reflexive mirror—an opportunity for a visitor to become entangled in the thoughts of her/his own and to reflect upon ruin metaphorically—revealing both familiar and unfamiliar histories of the self."[1]

The polarities which exist in ruined buildings of 'rampant destruction and defiant survival' echo in some way the human condition of psychological and physical decay matched with a stubborn and continuing existence (Fig.3). We can see ourselves in ruins. Perhaps the role of ruins is to remind us that even if we struggle in life, suffer loss and neglect and even injury and illness, we do often survive to become better and different beings as a result. Ruins are not to be pitied or feared; instead they need to be celebrated and have their stories woven, expressed and mused upon by their many onlookers and generally from such observers' subjective viewpoint. These musings can strongly influence new insights into the spectators' own psyches and the human condition in general.

Fig. 3 Chateau Villedieu

Also, Sigmund Freud's assertion that adult humans seek to disavow their own deaths may have some expression in ruined buildings. Ruinous landscapes indicate decay and desolation, but without the final end or natural conclusion, i.e. negation or death. Ruins, unlike humans do not die, they cannot, unless we kill them by destroying them completely and hauling off their component parts to make other useful buildings, which ironically means they will no longer be ruins anyway (Fig.4). In addition, in Fig.3 in Chapter 3, we can see a kind of post-death, which illuminates for us humans, the very real fear we have not just of death but of negation after death, a rotting of our flesh and bones, the need of our 'beings'. Interestingly though, ruins show us their

[1] Patrick Santoro, *With/In Ruin*, Carbondale, Illinois US, 2009, further reference, The Built, the Unbuilt and the Unbuildable: In *Pursuit of Architectural Meaning, Harbison, Robert, Cambridge*: MIT P, 1994

rotting, and their skeletal form (Fig.5), without actually dying. Ruins are alive by their very nature. Therefore, the human fascination for ruins may be an expression of and symbol for the 'mortal terror' we humans have of our own disease, decay, and death and this new 'post-death and decay.' As a result, ruins may be one of the fantastical solutions that only humans have an ability to arrange for themselves, in order to soothe the human consciousness around death. Such creating of ruins either by our willful destruction or neglect, may soothe and stroke our psyche and lead to an unconscious calming mechanism (Fig.6), as these conscious fears encapsulated in ruins are transferred into the unconscious mind. Ruins may assist us to place the conscious knowledge of our own demise in the 'zone of the hidden' or the 'unconscious'. Ruined buildings may be metaphors for our psychological deaths and the physical decay and death that we all experience, and they may help to keep such fears and anxieties at bay.

Fig.4 Chateau Villedieu

So our 'mortal terror' or fear of our own mortality, our going back to dust and decay, can perhaps be assuaged by these dreamy, ghost-like, brutal and romantic buildings. It seems they do have many uses and we must celebrate and save them for posterity and for future generations (Fig.7).

Fig. 5 Chateau Villedieu

Fig. 6 Chateau Villedieu

Fig. 7 Chateau Villedieu

Chapter 9 - The Social and Economic impact on Ruins

> *"Enhancing heritage is also a way to contribute to the revitalisation of city centres. City revitalisation is not only limited to a monument, but to a larger scope of old buildings (abandoned shipyards, industrial plants, old libraries, etc) that can be renovated and re-used for other purposes previously unforeseen. This in turn has many indirect socio-economic impacts and improves the area's image and reputation, which acts as a magnet to businesses."*[1]

This book has celebrated the romance, glory and historical value of ruins and also has debated the historical reasons for the existence of ruins in France and their historical and contemporary context in the wider world. This chapter focusses particularly on the political and practical imperatives which impact on the development and maintaining of a culture of ruination.

France is a huge country with vast open spaces and its many ruins have often been enabled and created by the Post-War culture of modernism and the French financial sector's favouring of new builds with better mortgage rates. (Fig.1, Fig.2) As a result, French people have chosen new housing, leaving a plethora of old, deserted or ruined buildings. These, taken as a whole, form a distinct iconic culture of ruination, made readily available to British and other *'etrangers'*, who have taken advantage of both freer movement within the European Union and, until recently, a strong exchange rate. This has enabled them to descend in droves onto the French countryside to renovate and restore even the most desolate of ruins, something that French people have found financially prohibitive and often incompatible with their own culture. (Fig. 3)

Fig.1 Ruined building on road to Levroux

[1] *Cultural Heritage as a Socio-Economic Development Factor, Archoimedes, 2005 (www.comune.venezia.it/flex/cm/pages/.../L/.../BLOB:ID%3D7755)*

Fig.2 Photo of new build, Rouvres Les Bois

Fig. 3 Restoration on a large house

Over the last few decades, *'etrangers'* from various parts of Europe and the US have made a concerted effort to build lives for themselves in France and in the process have saved ruins. (Fig.4). For instance, over 600,000 *'etrangers'* have come from the UK alone, it being a place which has a strong culture of restoration and renovation. Many ruins have been saved from destruction by the fanatical romantic desire in many English people to a) save 'the ruin' and b) engage in work on a spectrum from Do It Yourself to full on salvage and renovation. A tax credit on certain works on old buildings is also giving an imperative to such renovations.

Fig. 4 Restored house on way to Levroux

Fig.5 Deserted house and shop in Bouges Le Chateau, with for sale sign

There has also been, until recent times, a culture of renting homes for the French in France. This has begun to change as the result of *'etrangers'* ownership and renovations can be widely seen and be judged to be both a possibility and a desirable way to live. There seems to have been a change of heart in French people regarding the re-development of ruins, although some people may still view the determination of *'etrangers'* to own and restore as a kind of craziness akin to 'going out in the midday sun.' The restoration and renovation of ruins and their incorporation back into the community and landscape can be clearly seen now and is often acknowledged as a good thing. However, French people are often loathe to undertake such work either for cultural or financial reasons.. (Fig.5)

Fig. 6 Reclamation yard

There is a thriving architectural and structural reclamation (Fig. 6) economy in France. Obviously these '*originale*' items must come from somewhere to feed a stable growing market. Therefore ruined and deserted buildings can be also viewed as reclamation projects which provide a valuable resource to restorers of other ruins and a valuable source of income to the owners of ruins and reclamation yards alike. At the Chateau Le Pin, almost every interior fitting has been removed, presumably sold off or stolen for profit, thereby feeding into the reclamation culture. It is possible to see only a remnant now of a marvelous sweeping staircase, long since removed. (Fig.7)

Fig.7 Chateau Le Pin, interior with staircase

Interestingly, the Chateau de Veuil was turned into a ruin by Prince Tallyrand, who finding his chateau of Valencay in need of repair, decimated the chateau of Veuil to provide reclaimed materials for his house at Valencay. (Fig 8. and Fig. 9). This was a piece of systematic 'ruin making' born out of necessity as opposed to desertion.

The progression of planning laws and developments may also have had an effect both on the creation of ruins and the slow eroding of this culture of ruins through renovation and restoration. As mentioned already, in order to understand the French views about buying properties and renovating them, it is necessary to understand the way post World War 2 governments managed the housing problem. Their decision to build serial dwellings in big quantities and to rent them out meant that a very low number of families owned their own dwelling. Now the trend is turning to the opposite. It is easy to assume that everyone may favour this erosion of a culture of ruination, but it is not that simple.

As we have seen throughout this book, many people are in love with ruins and as such, the buildings themselves form a vital part of the wider culture in France and also their own discrete culturally iconic grouping. To lose all ruins would, I think, be a travesty and a desperate shame for French culture, which has for at least two centuries captured the imagination of people around the world, not least because of its idyllic ruins at once defiant and high-minded in their gentle slumber.

Fig 8 Veuil

Fig. 9 Valencay Chateau

Chapter 10 - Conclusion

> *"End, your dreamworld is just about to end,*
> *Fall, your dreamworld is just about to fall,*
> *Your dreamworld will fall"*[1]

Ruins are exciting, mysterious, sad for some and thrilling for others, but everyone has a view; ruins rarely evoke 'ambivalence'. Opinions usually range from a desire to preserve and even rebuild, thereby negating the building's purpose as a ruin through to the strident demand to 'demolish' or '*demolir'*. Ruins can in turn fulfill us and repel us, and in some way this book seeks to understand the ruin, for what it is: cultural icon, personal saviour, mirror of the times, joy to behold or even irritation.

This book has attempted to discuss and explain ruins and the culture of ruined buildings. It stands as a memorial to those brave buildings holding on to life as buildings and in some cases without even a semblance of a building at all, and yet is still a live ruin. It is hoped in bringing these buildings to people's attention, that of course some may be saved and restored to former glory, but there is scope still for many of these beautiful and mysterious buildings to live on as ruins.

The psychology of ruins has also been explored, which gives some clues as to the future of the culture of ruins. We need ruins it seems, to assist us in our journey through life; they provide a powerful enlightenment to and place of safe keeping from our fears of decay and mortality. In our ever changing world it is also clear that ruins will persist as cultural icons and that to sweep away such desolated buildings is a mistake: a denial of our cultural heritage. A nation might worry if its material world is a) disposable because of a lack of quality in design and construction and b) so afraid of its own cultural and historical shadow that demolition is the only option. Thankfully France has neither of these aspects in its toolkit for urban and rural development. In fact, it seems to be so at one with its history and design as to be easily able to accommodate a wealth of ruins and not to feel threatened by them and what they signify.

The book has covered the various types of buildings that may be ruinous and in this chapter a further selection of buildings are displayed with very short descriptions. This selection is a microcosm of the whole book, as it covers all of the types of building mentioned therein.

Windmill, northern France (Fig. 1)
This windmill sits alone in a field.

[1] Midnight Oil, *Diesel and Dust*, lyrics, 1988 (www.auralgasms.com/radio/Lyric1160.aspx)

War pictures (Fig. 2, 3, 4, 5, 6 & 7)
Images of ruination from the First World

23. BORDEAUX. — Les ruines du Palais Gallien
W. F.
DÉPOSÉ

L'AUVERGNE PITTORESQUE
508. Ruines du Château de MUROLS
Construit à 929 m. d'altitude sur un cône basaltique, était autrefois le " Méroliacense Castrum " qui soutint un siège en l An 532 contre Thierry. Toute la partie Ouest est antérieure au XIVe siècle; les autres parties sont des XIVe et XVe siècles.

Omecourt Chateau (Fig. 8)
A large chateau privately owned but practically deserted and decaying.

Ruined house in Valencay (Fig. 9)
A small farmhouse, now decaying and used a a giant hay store and stable for a horse.

Deserted house in Cormery (Fig. 10)
Tiny house in the shadow of Abbaye de Cormery, probably attached to the Abbaye.

A drive through France, taking in any region or department will bring pleasure to the ruined building enthusiast. It is a unique country, one which actively maintains its ruination culture, rather than simply neglects its ruins. Some owners may be ashamed of the fact that they have let often great buildings decay and fall, but they need not be embarrassed, for their inability or reluctance to maintain their homes and businesses provides France with major cultural icons and places of comfort and consolation to those who are battered and bruised by life. This book is a celebration of this rebellious determination of old and tired buildings to repose in faded splendour.